for 1000+ tutorials ... use our
free site .... drawinghowtodraw.com

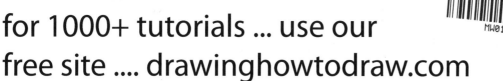

MW01114594

BY RACHEL GOLDSTEIN

DRAWING CHIBI SUPERCUTE CHARACTERS

EASY FOR BEGINNERS & KIDS (MANGA / ANIME)

LEARN HOW TO DRAW CUTE CHIBIS IN ANIMAL ONESIES WITH THEIR KAWAII PETS

CUTE PANDAS

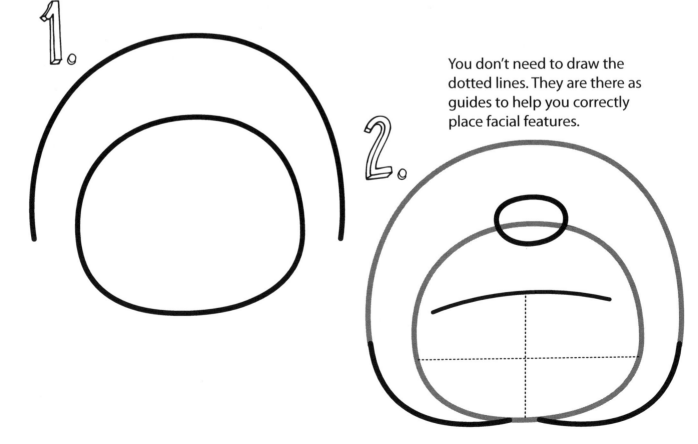

You don't need to draw the dotted lines. They are there as guides to help you correctly place facial features.

3.

Letter "C" Ears

Draw the Letters "LOL"

Erase on dotted line

4.

5.

Letter "V" shapes

Erase on dotted line

6.

Letter "L"
Arms

Erase
on
dotted
lines

7.

Letter "D"
Snout

Letter "C"
Feet

8.

CUTE MONKEYS

1.

2.

Letter "C" Ears

3.

Letters "C" + "W"

4.

Letter "S"-like Curve

You don't need to draw the dotted lines. They are there as guides to help you correctly place facial features.

5.

#75 shape

6.

"V" shapes

#3 shape

7.

8.

Sideways
"?"-like
shape

Erase
on
dotted
lines

9.

CUTE LIONS

1.

2.

Letter "V"-like ears

Draw
Some
Letter "M"
Zig-zags

You don't need to draw the dotted lines. They are there as guides to help you correctly place facial features.

3.

Letters "VOW"

4.

↑
#3 Shapes

5. Draw zig-zags around the head.

6.

7.

"V" Shaped
Eye Lashes

"G" shapes →

8.

Erase
on
Dotted
Lines

Letter
"M"
Shapes

Sideways
"?"
Shape

9.

10.

11.

12.

CUTE KANGAROOS

1.

2.

You don't need to draw the dotted lines. They are there as guides to help you correctly place facial features.

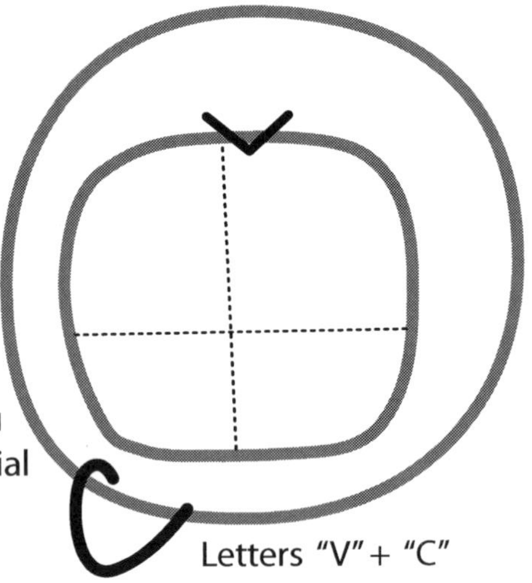

Letters "V" + "C"

3.

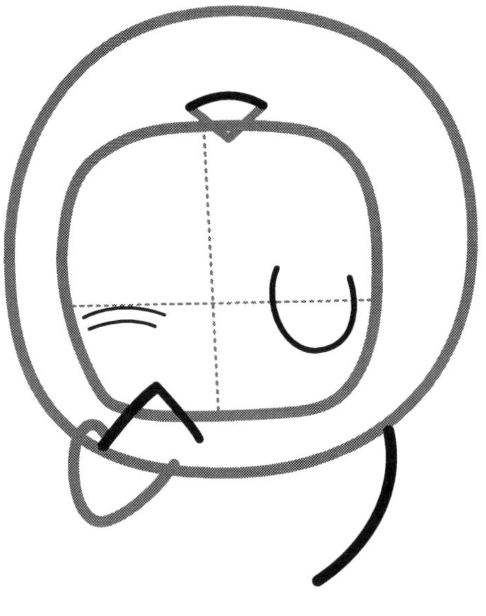

4.

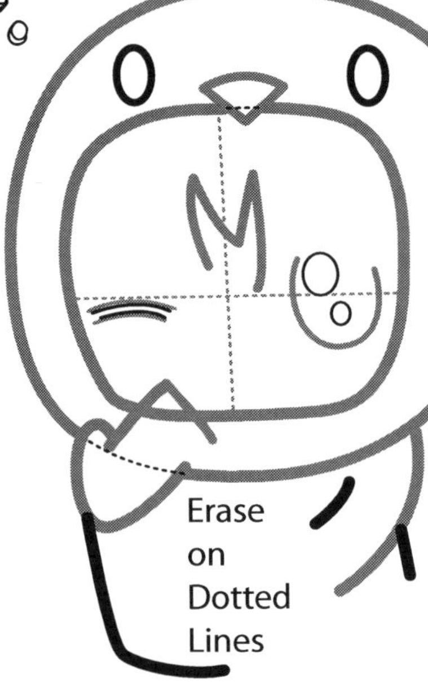

Erase on Dotted Lines

5.

Upside Down
"V" Shape

Sideways
"?" Shape

6.

"M"
Shape

Erase
on the
Dotted
Line

7.

8.

9.

CUTE DUCKS

1.

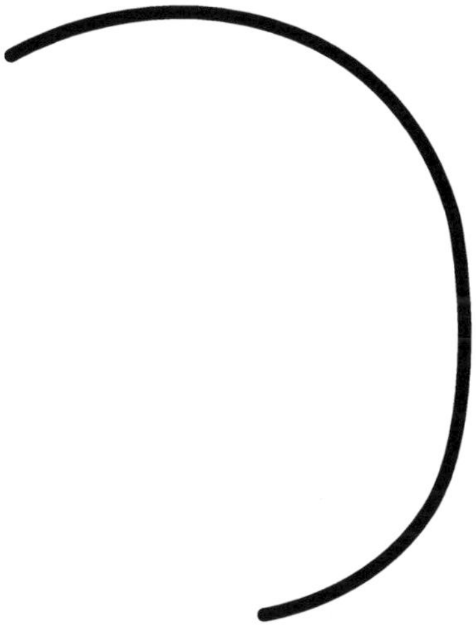

2.

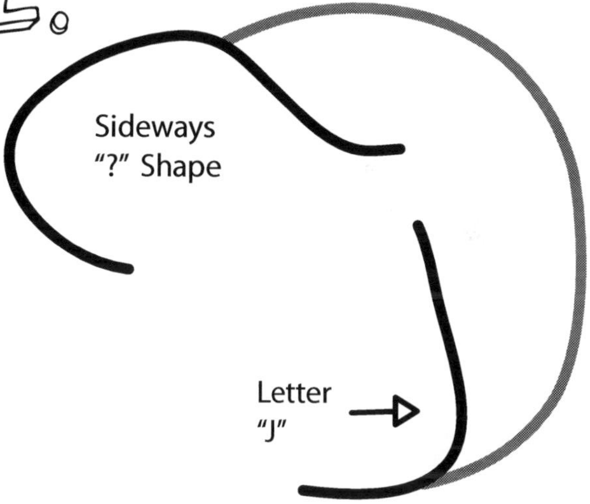

Sideways
"?" Shape

Letter
"J" →

3.

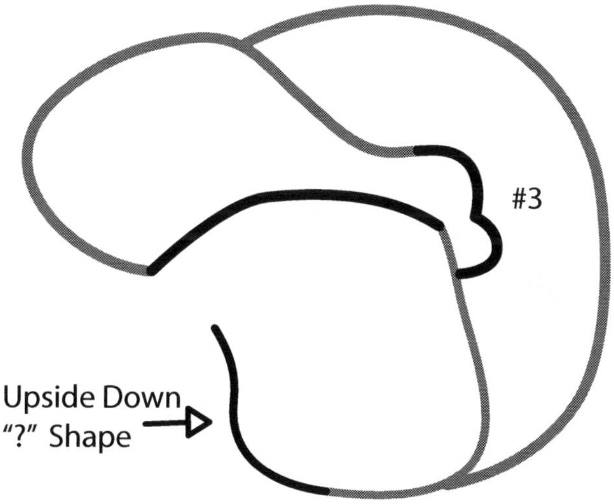

Upside Down →
"?" Shape

#3

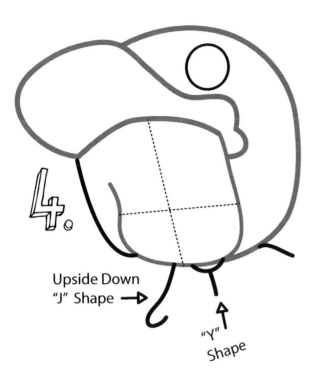

4.

Upside Down "J" Shape →

↑ "Y" Shape

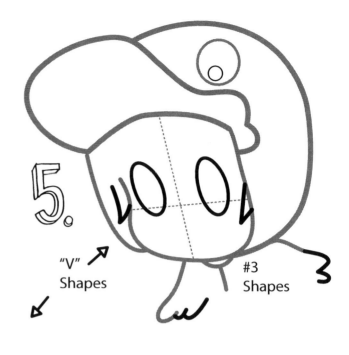

5.

"V" Shapes ↗

↙

#3 Shapes

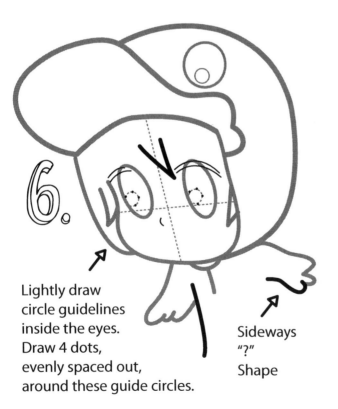

6.

Lightly draw circle guidelines inside the eyes. Draw 4 dots, evenly spaced out, around these guide circles.

Sideways "?" Shape

7.

"W" + "Z" Shapes

Connect the dots (that you drew in Step #6) by turning them into letter "V" shapes

Letter "S" Shape

8.

Connect the
remaining dots
with a letter
"V" shape and
2 lines.

9.

#3 →

Upside
Down
"?"
Shapes

10.

#3 + "L"
Shapes

CUTE DOLPHIN

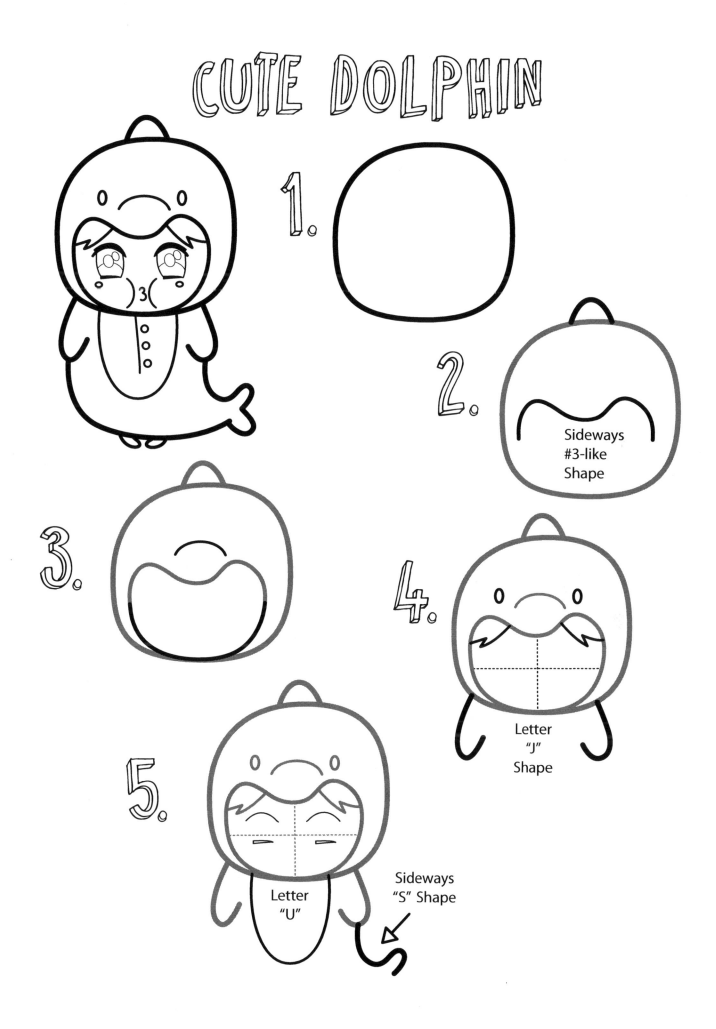

1.

2. Sideways #3-like Shape

3.

4. Letter "J" Shape

5. Letter "U"

Sideways "S" Shape

6.

#3
Shape

3

7.

Erase
on
Dotted
Lines

3

Letter
"Z"
Shapes

8.

3

CUTE BEARS

1.

2.

3

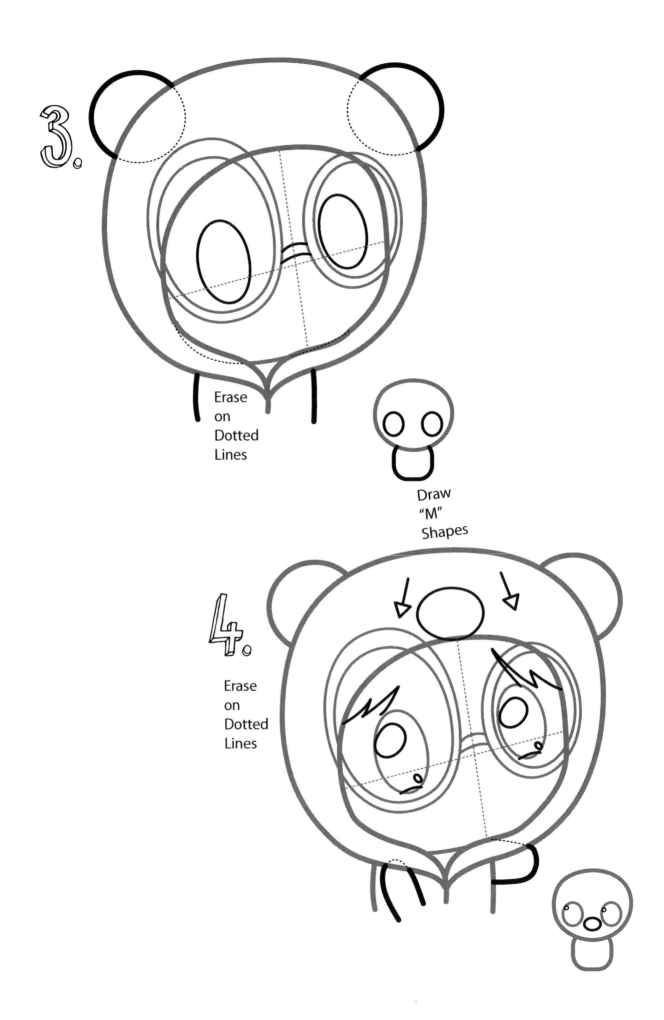

3.

Erase
on
Dotted
Lines

Draw
"M"
Shapes

4.

Erase
on
Dotted
Lines

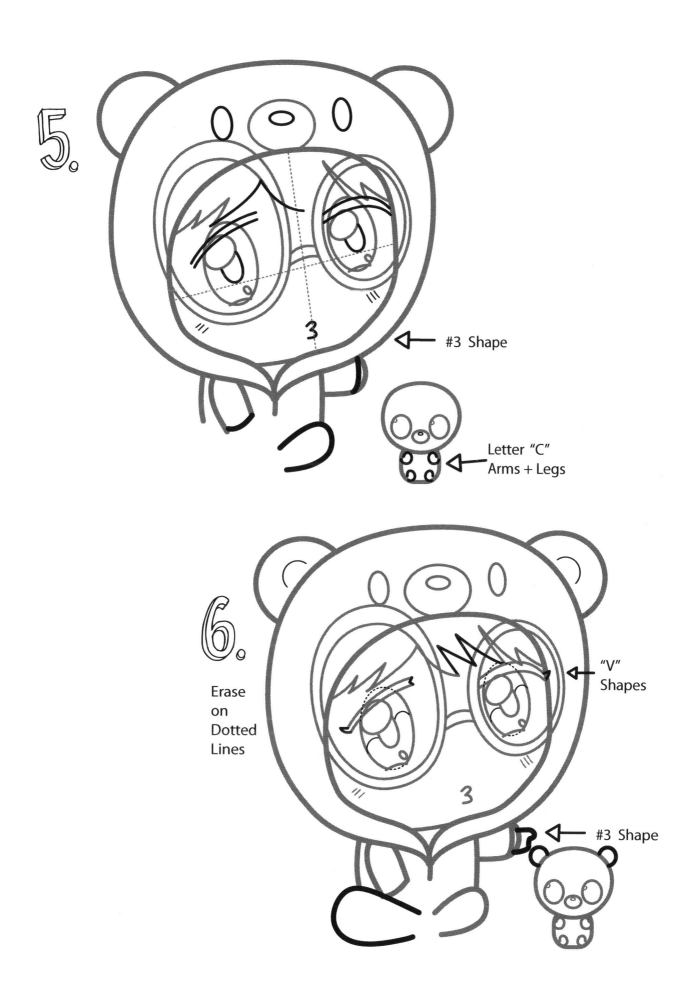

5.

#3 Shape

Letter "C"
Arms + Legs

6.

Erase
on
Dotted
Lines

"V"
Shapes

3

#3 Shape

CUTE UNICORNS

1.

Upside
Down
"?"
Shape

2.

3.

4.

5.

6.

Letter "V" Shapes

7.

"V"
Shapes

#3 Shapes

8.

Erase
on
Dotted
Lines

Draw
a
Wiggly
Line for
the Mane

#3 Shapes →

"J" and "C" →
Shapes

CUTE UNICORNS

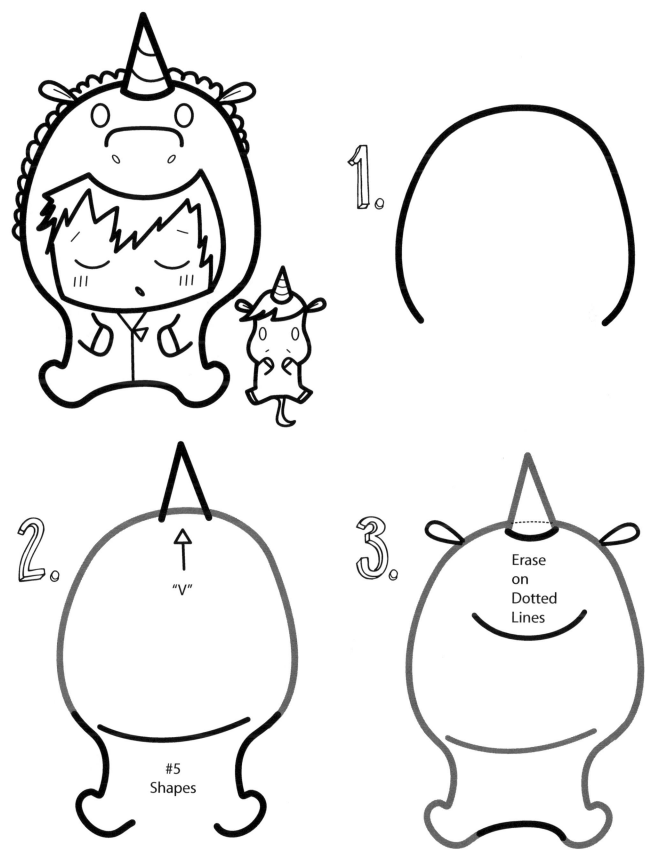

1.

2.

"V"

#5
Shapes

3.

Erase
on
Dotted
Lines

4.

Upside Down "?" Shapes

Letter "Y" Shape

5.

Zig-zag Hair

"R"-like Shapes for Arms

"V" + "M" Shapes

6.

Wiggly Lines for the Mane

Letter "S" Shape

CUTE DOGS

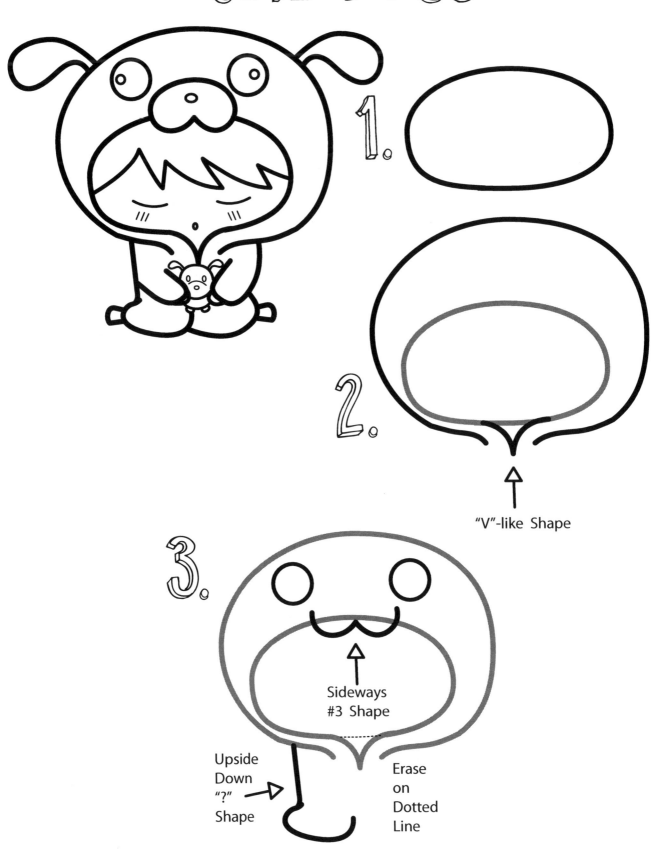

1.

2. "V"-like Shape

3. Sideways #3 Shape

Upside Down "?" Shape

Erase on Dotted Line

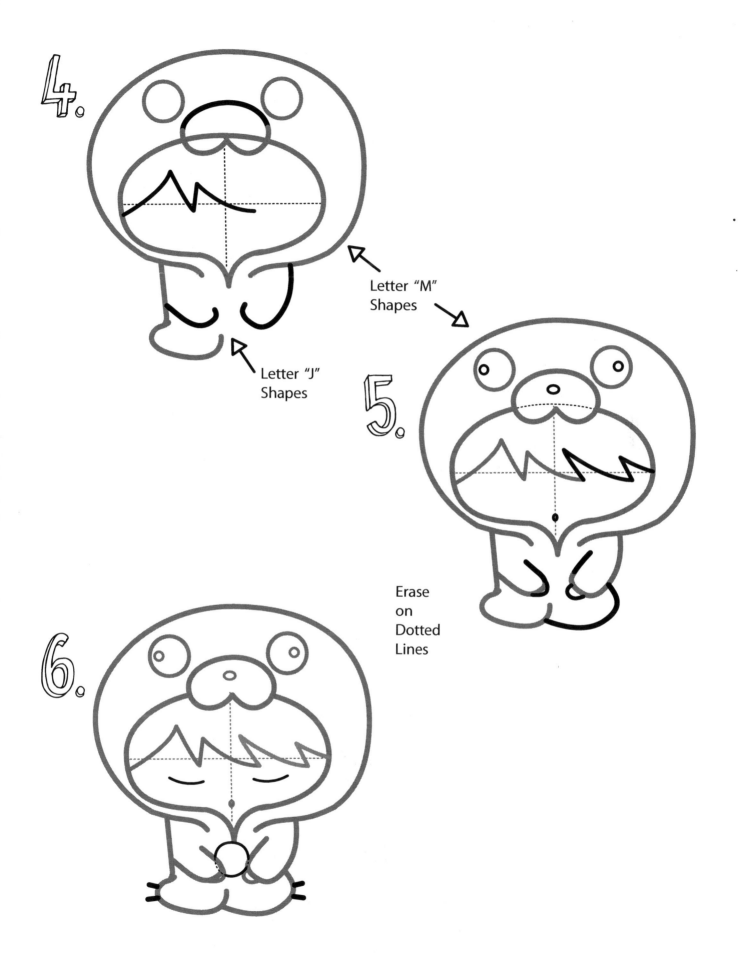

4.

Letter "M" Shapes

Letter "J" Shapes

5.

Erase
on
Dotted
Lines

6.

7.

Sideways
"?" Shapes

8.

9.

CUTE RACCOONS

1.

Sideways
#3 Shape

2.

3.

Draw 2 Upside Down
Letter "J" Shapes

4.

"W"-Like
Shapes

"?"-Like
Shape

5.

6.

Letter
"V"-Like
Ears + Arms

"?"-Like
Shapes

7.

Letter
"V"
Shapes

#3

Erase
on
Dotted
Lines

Upside Down
"?" Shapes

8.

9.

CUTE BUNNIES

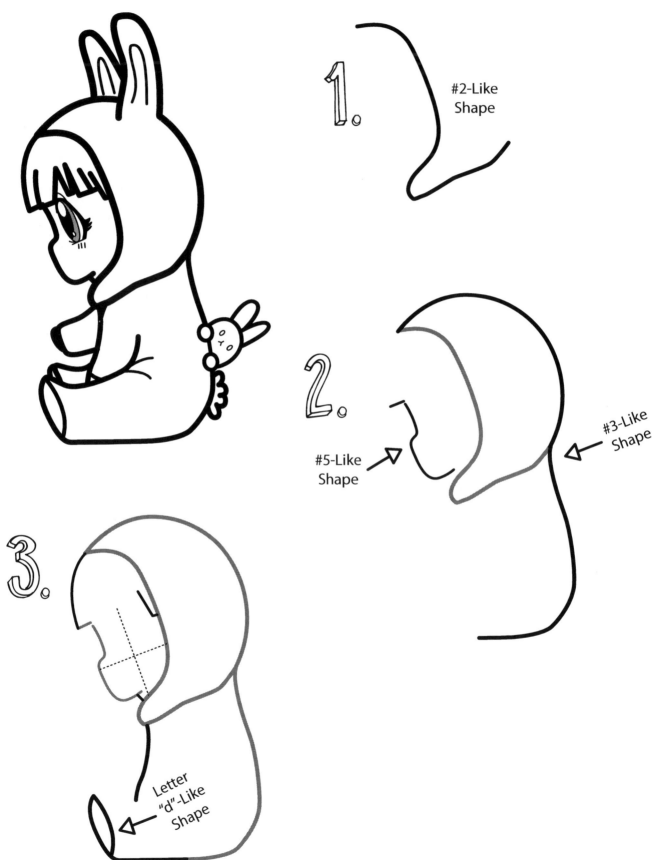

1. #2-Like Shape

2. #5-Like Shape   #3-Like Shape

3. Letter "d"-Like Shape

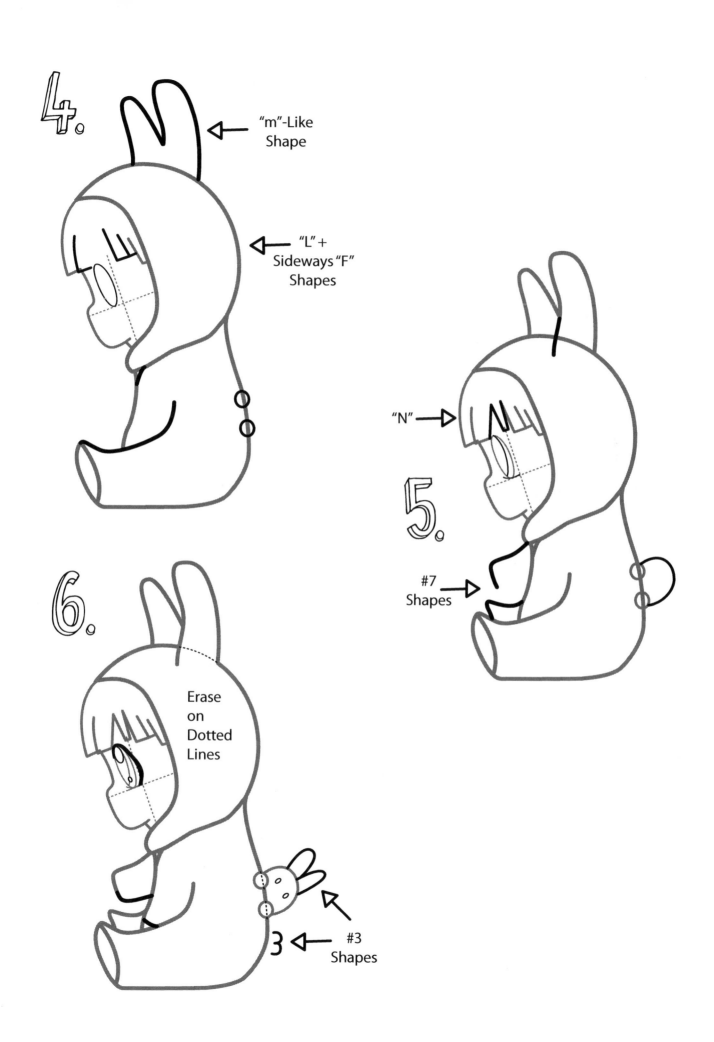

4.

"m"-Like Shape

"L" + Sideways "F" Shapes

5.

"N"

#7 Shapes

6.

Erase on Dotted Lines

3

#3 Shapes

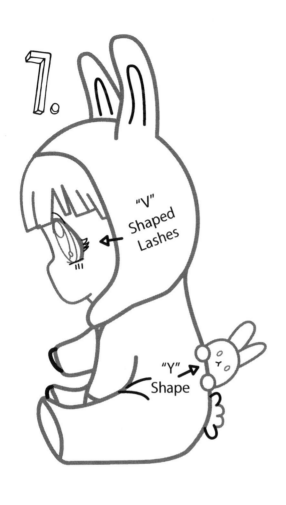

7.

"V"
Shaped
Lashes

"Y"
Shape

8.

CUTE TIGER

1.

2.

3.

4.

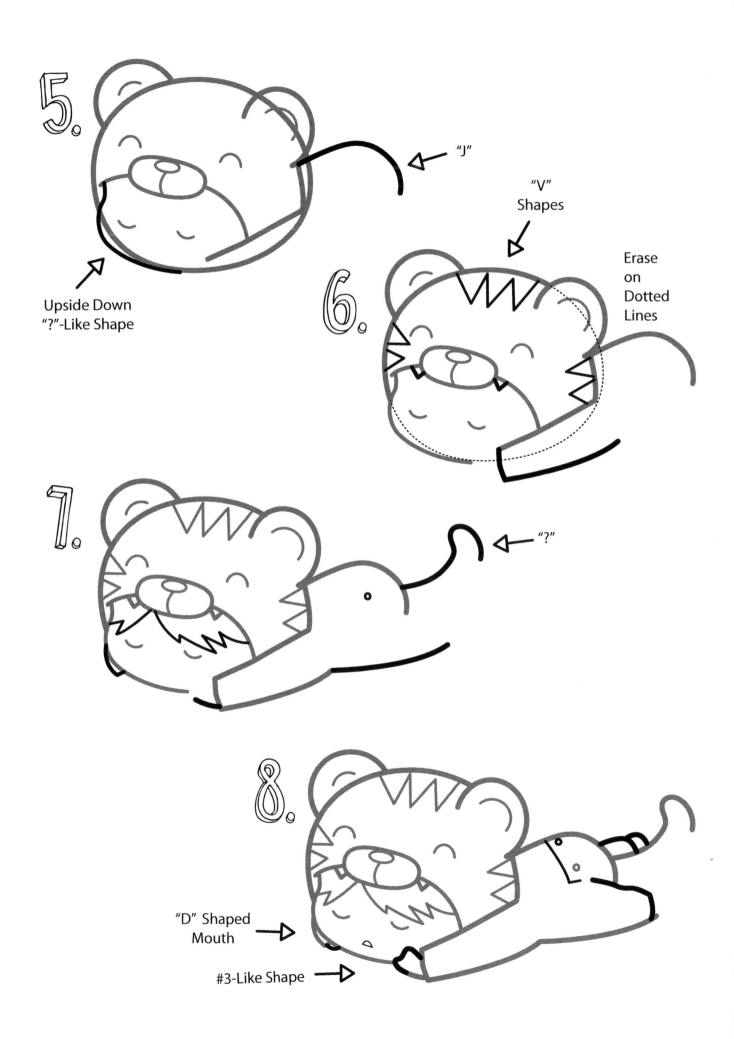

5.

"J"

Upside Down
"?"-Like Shape

"V"
Shapes

Erase
on
Dotted
Lines

6.

7.

"?"

8.

"D" Shaped
Mouth

#3-Like Shape

9.

#3-Like
Shape

10.

"V"
Shapes

11.

CUTE FROGS

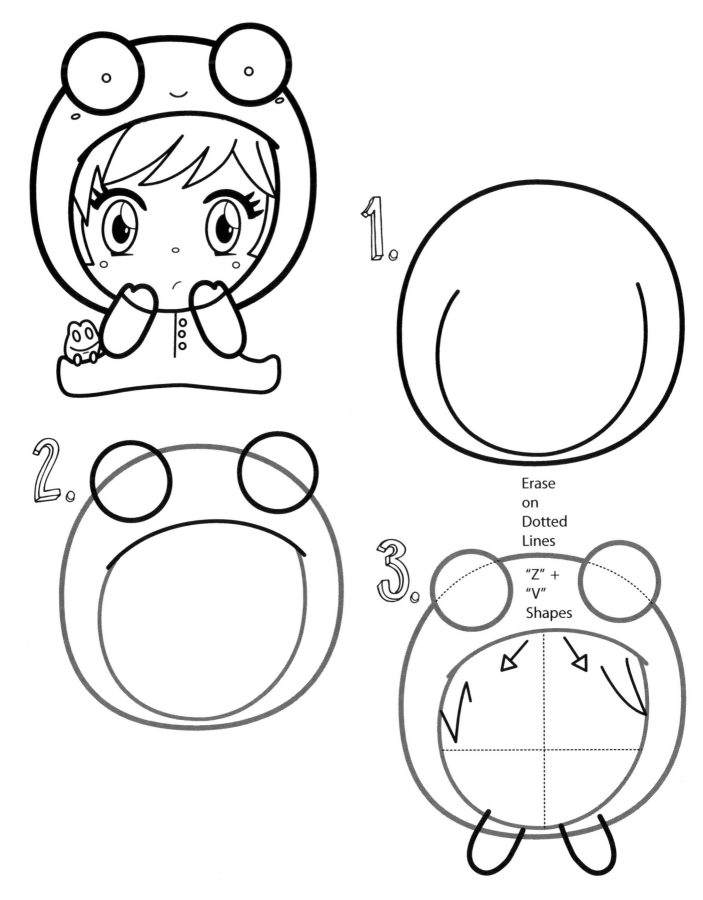

1.

2.

3.

Erase on Dotted Lines

"Z" + "V" Shapes

4.

"W"

#3 Shapes

"?" Shapes

5.

"V" + "L" Shapes

Erase on Dotted Lines

6.

"V"-Shaped Eye Lashes

#3 Shape

7.

Erase
on
Dotted
Lines

8.

CUTE DINOSAURS

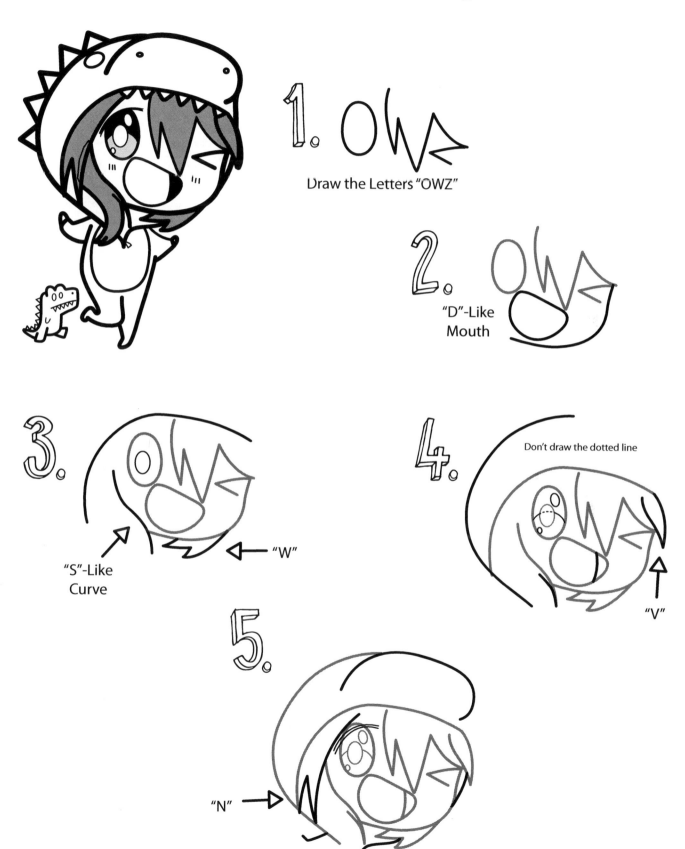

1. OWZ
Draw the Letters "OWZ"

2. "D"-Like Mouth

3. "S"-Like Curve   "W"

4. Don't draw the dotted line   "V"

5. "N"

6. "v"

"e" + "W"
Shapes

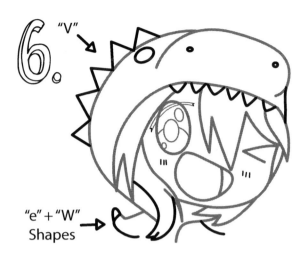

7.

Erase
on
Dotted
Lines

"S"-Like Shape

#9

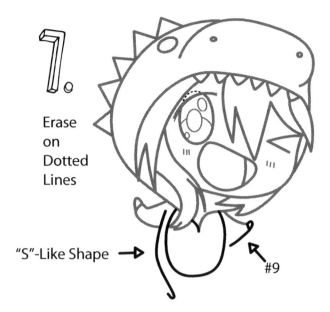

8.

9.

#3 + #5
Shapes

10.

"S"-Like
Shape

11.

12.

CUTE DRAGON

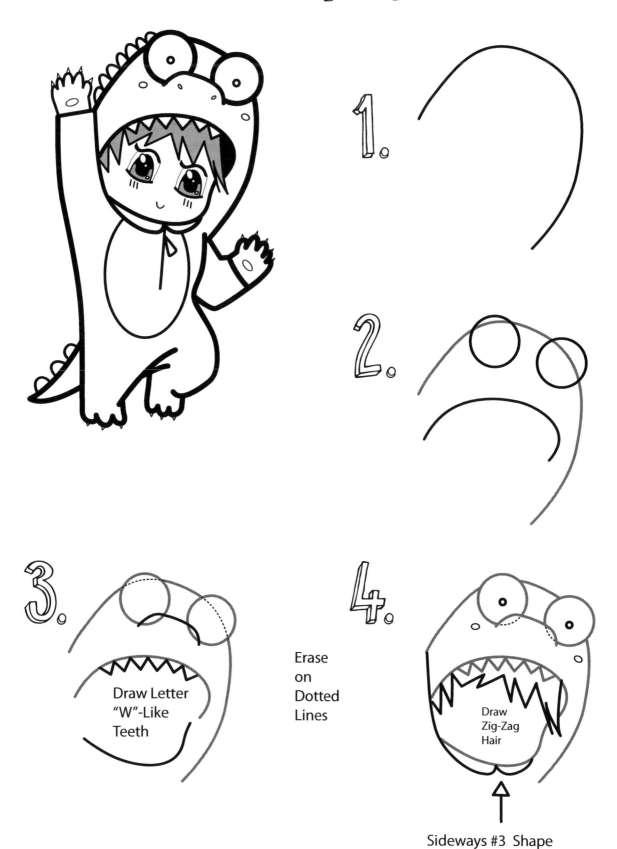

1.

2.

3. Draw Letter "W"-Like Teeth

Erase on Dotted Lines

4. Draw Zig-Zag Hair

Sideways #3 Shape

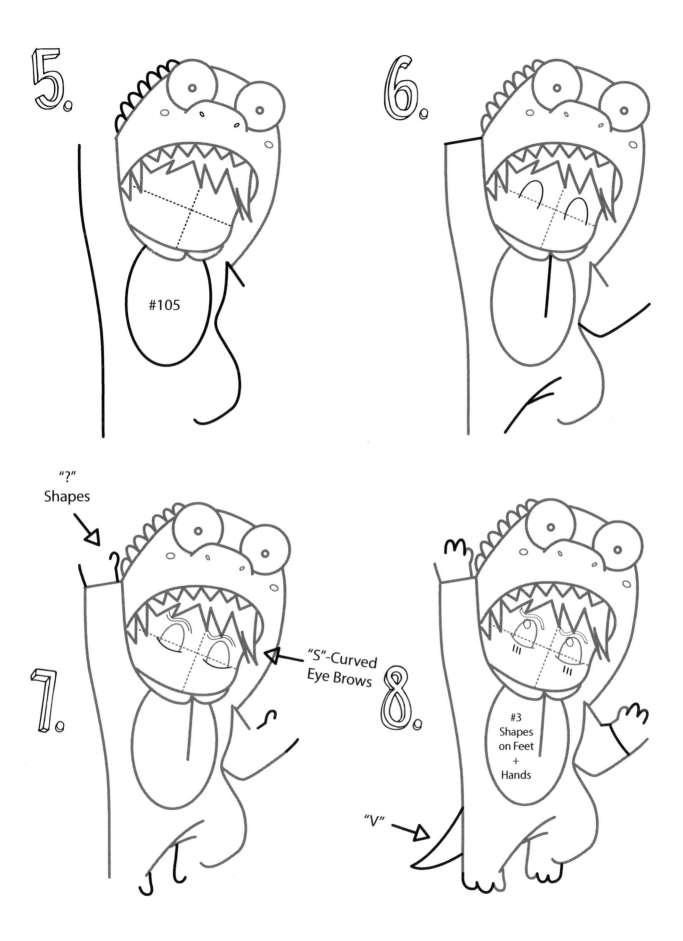

9. Erase on Dotted Lines

#3 Shapes

10.

Draw "V" Shaped Claws

11.

12.

CUTE GIRAFFES

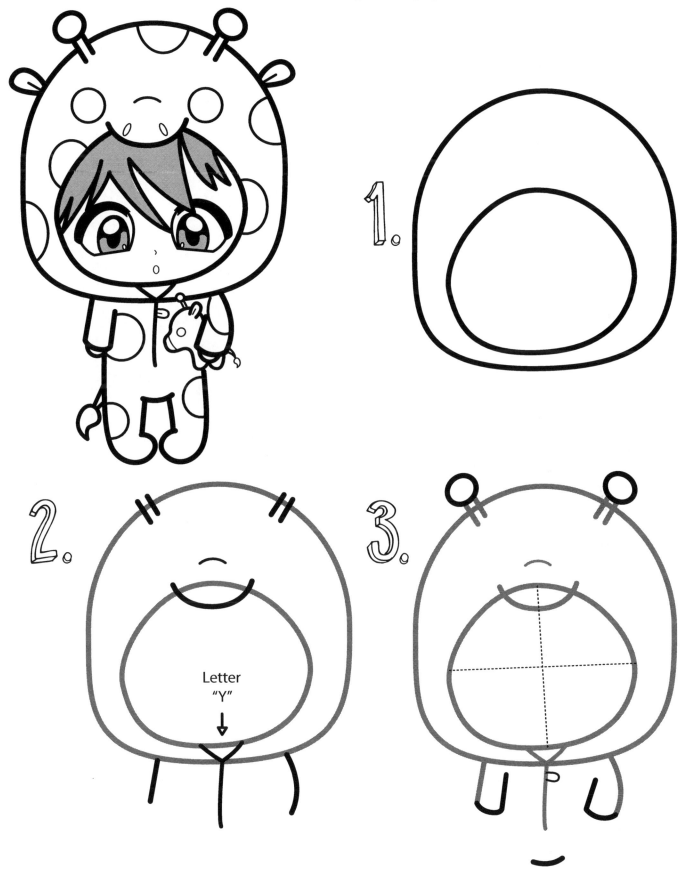

1.

2. Letter "Y"

3.

7.

"W" Shape

"?" + "S" Shapes

8.

9.

CUTE PIGS

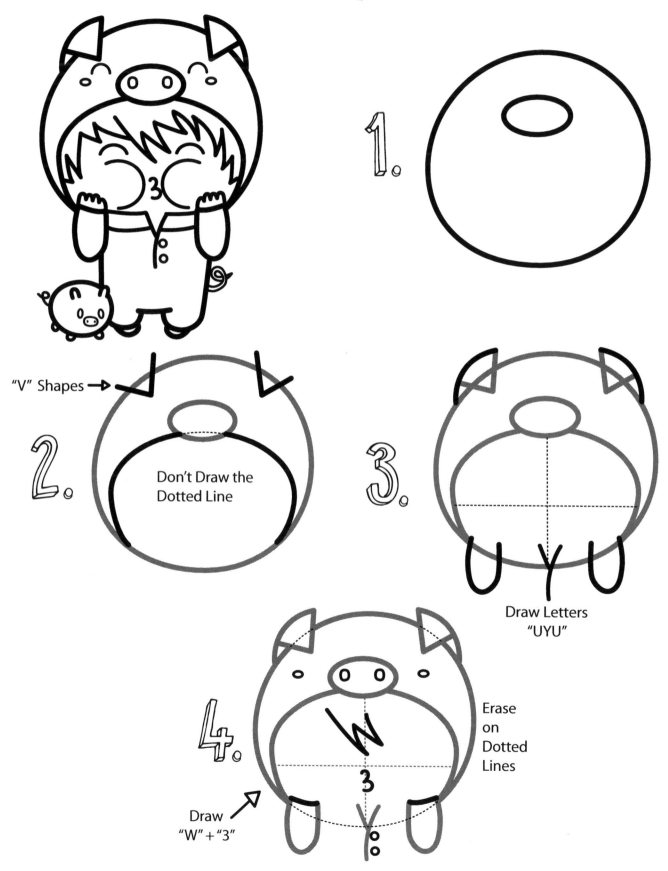

1.

"V" Shapes →

2.

Don't Draw the Dotted Line

3.

Draw Letters "UYU"

4.

Draw "W" + "3"

Erase on Dotted Lines

5.

Draw Letter
"C" Cheeks
+ Eyes

6.

#3 Shapes

"J" Shaped
Legs

Don't Draw the
Dotted Line

7.

Draw Cursive
Letter "e" Tails

8.

Erase
on
Dotted
Line

Draw Cursive
Letter "e" Tails

9.

CUTE REINDEER

1.

2.

3.

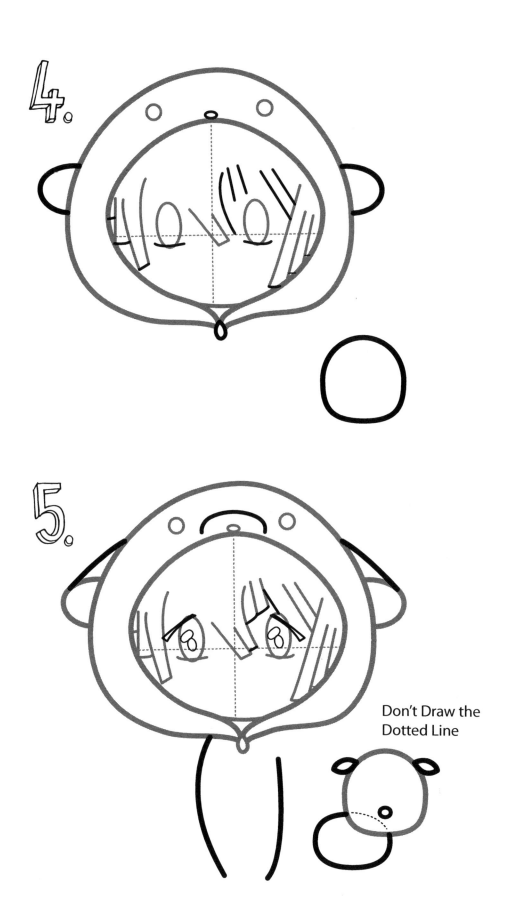

4.

5.

Don't Draw the
Dotted Line

6.

#3
Shapes

"?"-Like
Shapes
for Antlers
+ Feet

7.

Erase
on
Dotted
Lines

CUTE OWLS

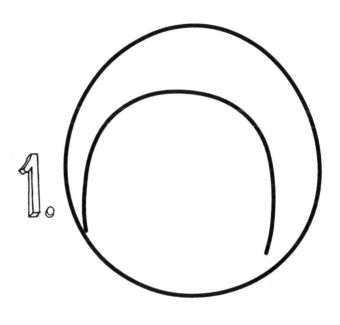

1.

Erase
on
Dotted
Lines

2.

3.

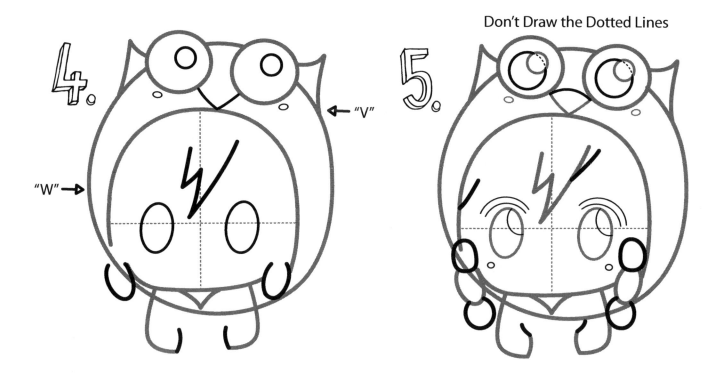

4.

"V"

"W"

Don't Draw the Dotted Lines

5.

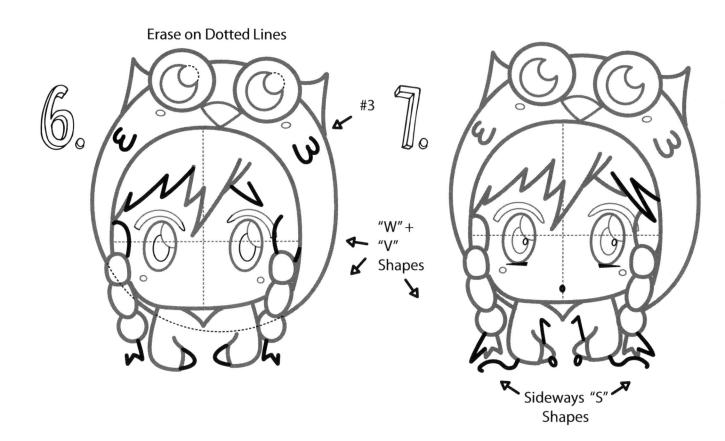

Erase on Dotted Lines

6.

ε   3

#3

"W" +
"V"
Shapes

7.

ε   3

Sideways "S"
Shapes

8.

"V" Shaped Lashes

"S" Shaped Feet

9.

10.

CUTE MICE

1.

2.

3.

4.

"M" + "V" Shapes

5.

#8
Shapes

← "?" Shapes

6.

Erase
on
Dotted
Lines

Letter "C"
Shaped
Fingers + Ears

7.

8.

CUTE CATS

1.

2.

"V" + "W" Shapes

3.

"?" Shapes

4.

"W", "U", + "D" Shapes

"S" →

#3

5.

"V" Ears

6.

Erase
on
Dotted
Lines

CUTE PENGUINS

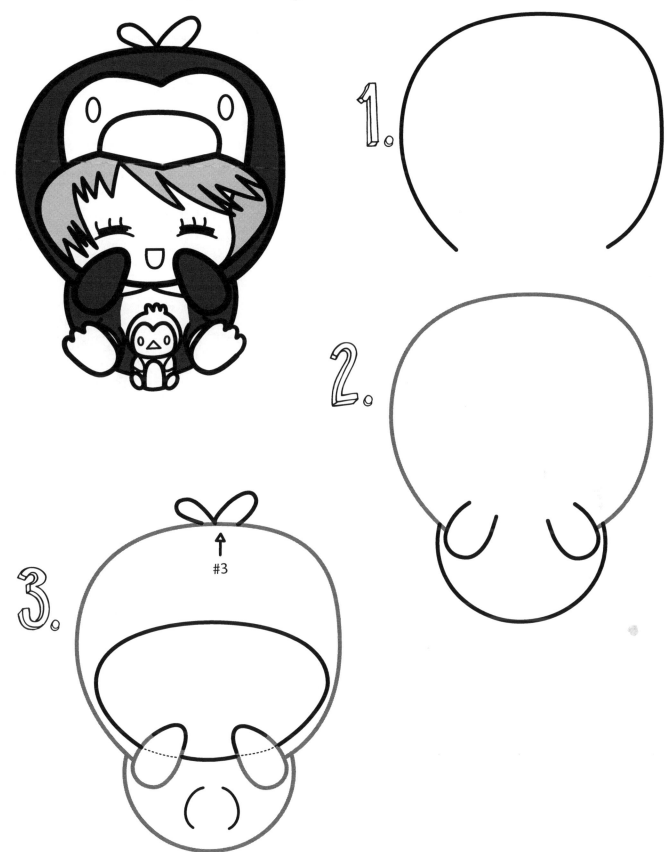

1.

2.

3.

#3

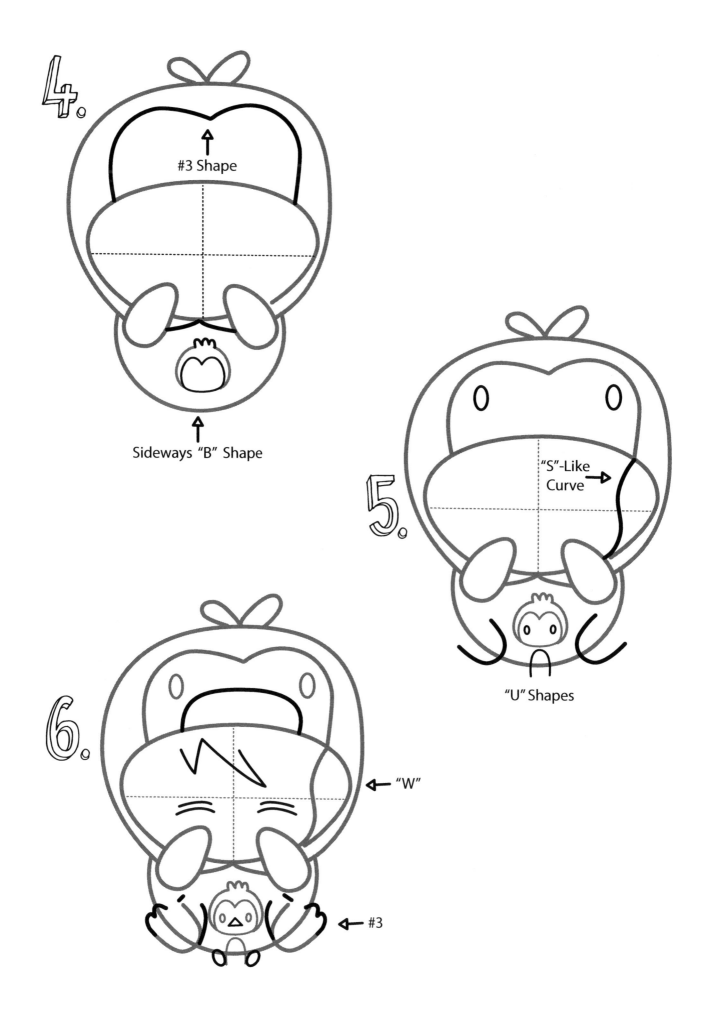

4.

#3 Shape

Sideways "B" Shape

5.

"S"-Like Curve

"U" Shapes

6.

"W"

#3

7.

8.

Erase
on
Dotted
Lines

9.

CUTE CATS

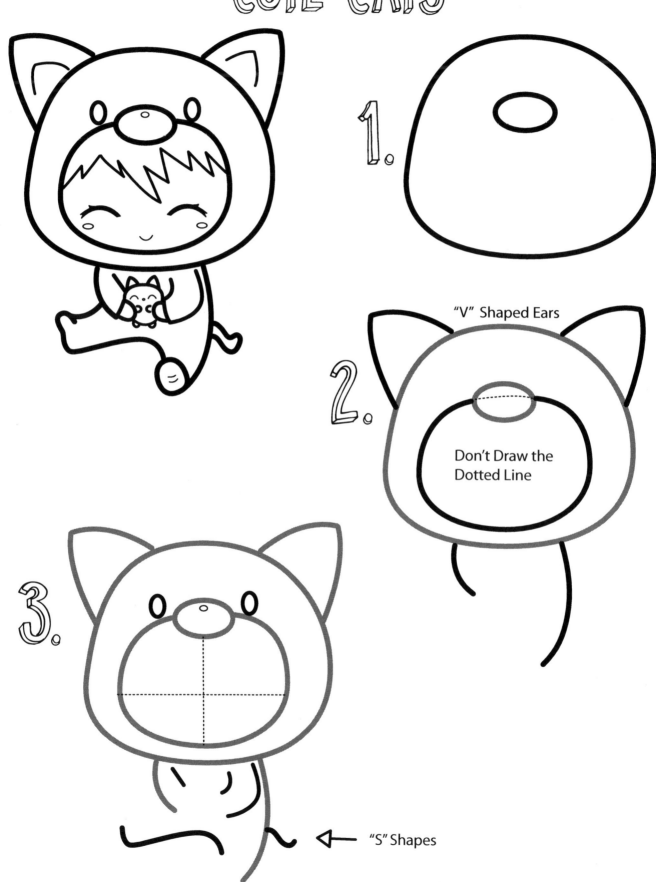

1.

2. "V" Shaped Ears

Don't Draw the Dotted Line

3.

← "S" Shapes

4.

Letters "MWM"

#3 Like Shape

5.

6.

"V" + "U" Shapes

7.

8.

CUTE SHARKS

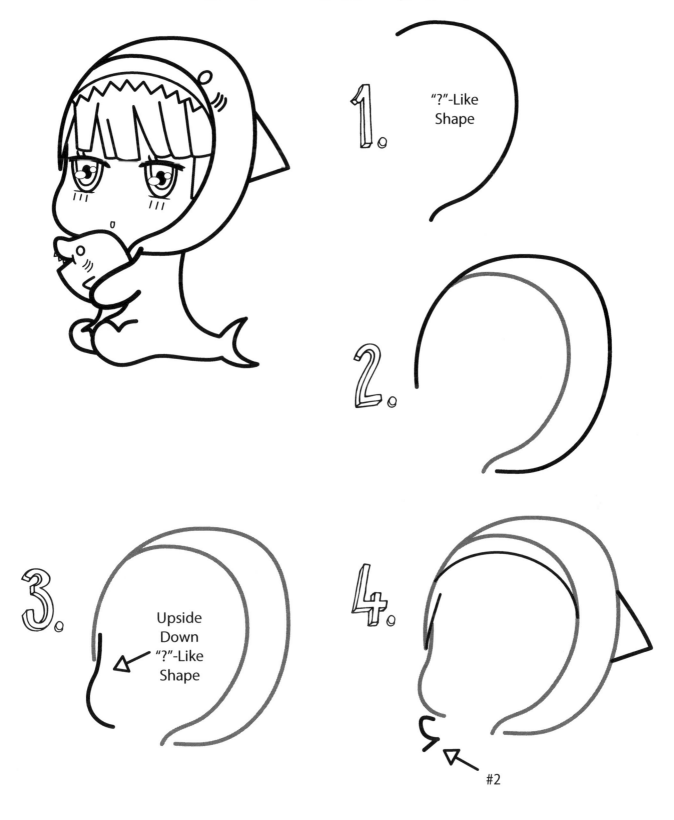

1. "?"-Like Shape

2.

3. Upside Down "?"-Like Shape

4. #2

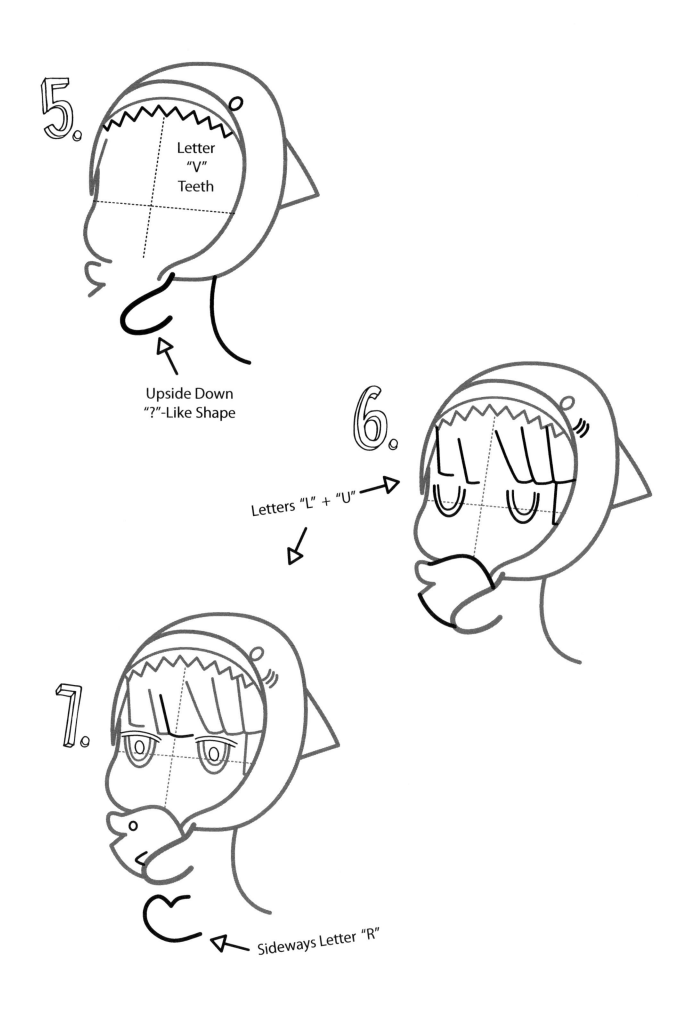

5.

Letter "V" Teeth

Upside Down "?"-Like Shape

6.

Letters "L" + "U"

7.

Sideways Letter "R"

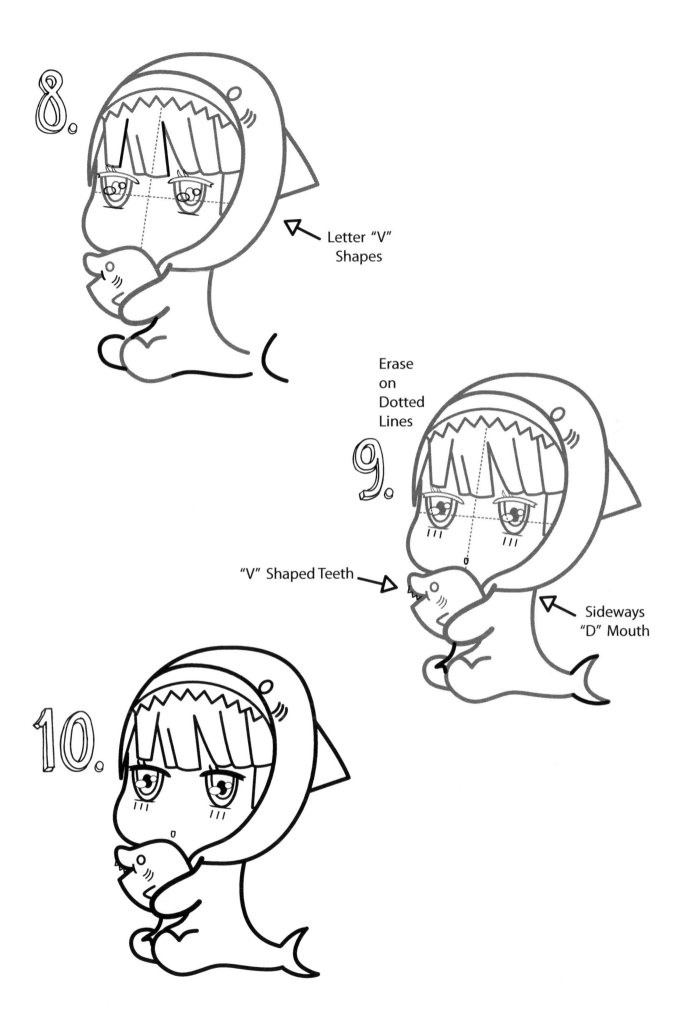

8.

Letter "V"
Shapes

Erase
on
Dotted
Lines

9.

"V" Shaped Teeth

Sideways
"D" Mouth

10.

A FEW FREE PAGES FROM MY KAWAII DRAWING BOOKS

HOW to DRAW KAWAII CUTE ANIMALS and CHARACTERS

DRAWING for KIDS with LETTERS NUMBERS and SHAPES

CARTOONING FOR KIDS AND LEARNING HOW TO DRAW CUTE KAWAII ANIMALS AND CHARACTERS WITH ALPHABET LETTERS, NUMBERS, AND SHAPES

BY RACHEL GOLDSTEIN

HOW to DRAW KAWAII CUTE ANIMALS · CHARACTERS 3

EASY to DRAW ANIME and MANGA DRAWING for KIDS

CARTOONING FOR KIDS · LEARNING HOW TO DRAW SUPER CUTE KAWAII ANIMALS, CHARACTERS, DOODLES, & THINGS

BY RACHEL GOLDSTEIN

HOW to DRAW KAWAII CUTE ANIMALS · CHARACTERS 2

EASY to DRAW ANIME and MANGA DRAWING for KIDS

CARTOONING FOR KIDS · LEARNING HOW TO DRAW SUPER CUTE KAWAII ANIMALS, CHARACTERS, DOODLES, & THINGS

BY RACHEL GOLDSTEIN

KISSING KITTIES

1.

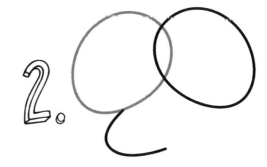

2.

Letter "V" ears

Don't draw the dotted line

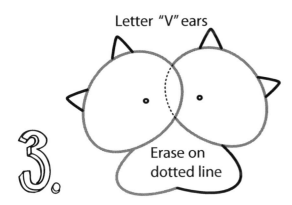

3.

Erase on dotted line

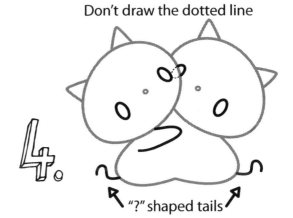

4.

"?" shaped tails

Letter "V" shape

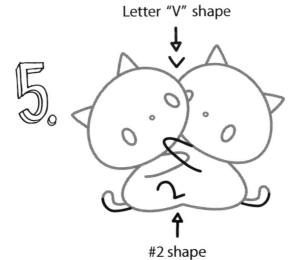

5.

#2 shape

6.

#3 shapes

Backwards #2 shape

Erase
on
dotted
lines

7.

NOW YOU TRY

DOG IN SHARK HAT

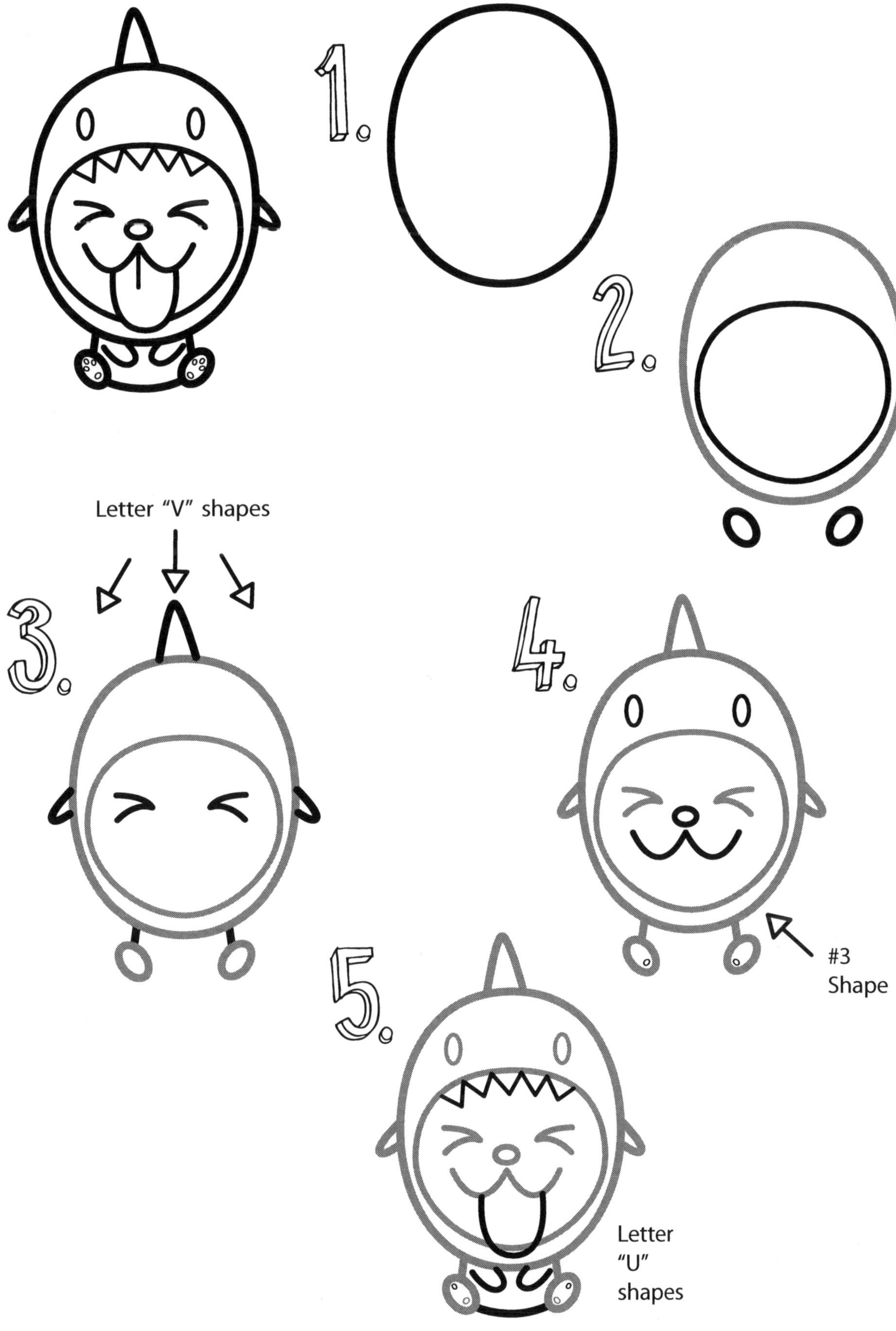

1.

2.

3.

Letter "V" shapes

4.

#3 Shape

5.

Letter "U" shapes

6.

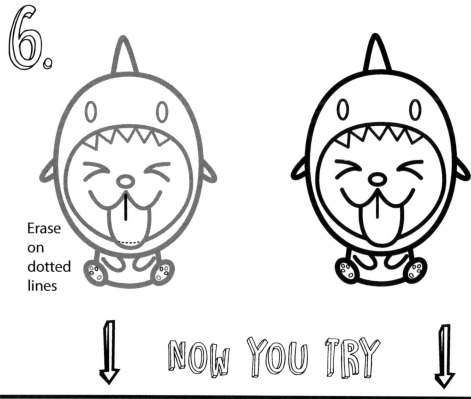

Erase on dotted lines

NOW YOU TRY

A FEW FREE PAGES FROM MY COOL STUFF BOOKS

BOY PUSHING ELEPHANT OFF OF PAPER

Here is another cool paper folding-over project. Draw an elephant on one side of the page and a boy on the other. When you fold it over, you have the boy pushing the elephant.

1. First of all, you need to draw a cartoon boy on the right side of a piece of paper turned on its side. I will show you how to draw him below.

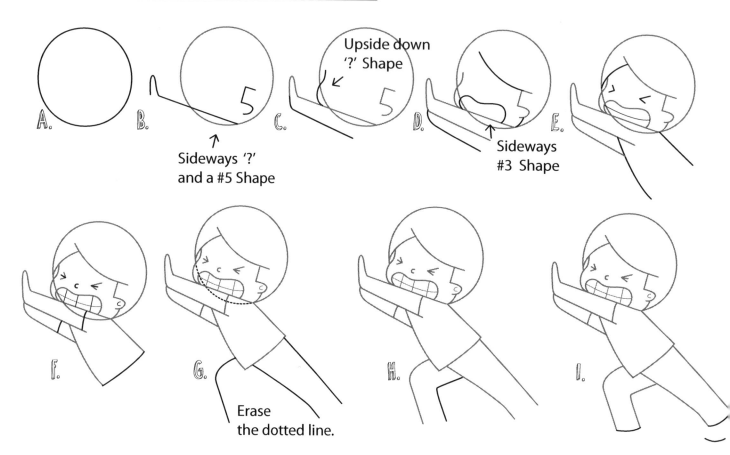

A.

B.
Sideways '?' and a #5 Shape

C.
Upside down '?' Shape

D.
Sideways #3 Shape

E.

F.

G.
Erase the dotted line.

H.

I.

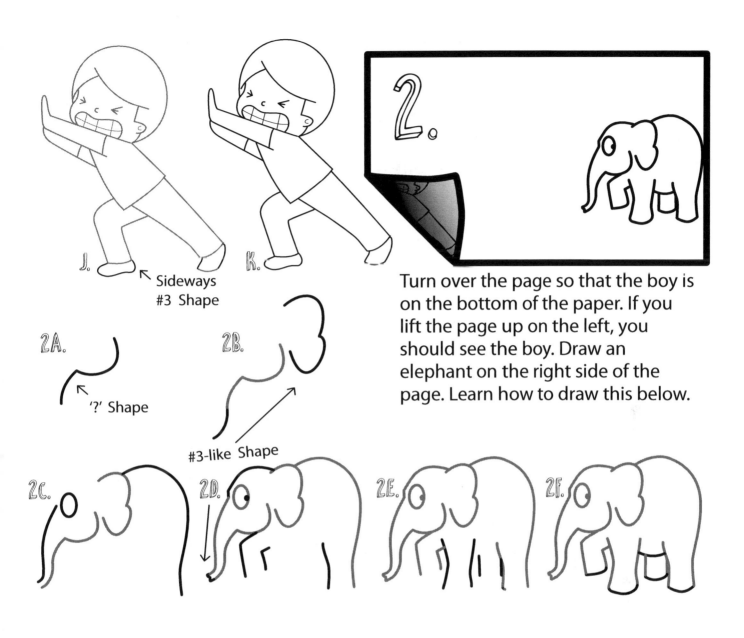

J.

← Sideways #3 Shape

K.

2.

Turn over the page so that the boy is on the bottom of the paper. If you lift the page up on the left, you should see the boy. Draw an elephant on the right side of the page. Learn how to draw this below.

2A.

← '?' Shape

2B.

#3-like Shape

2C.

2D.

2E.

2F.

3.

Now roll / curve the paper over and match up the boy's hands with the elephant. It will look like the kid is pushing the elephant off of the paper. Really cool!

BOX RISING OFF OF PAPER

Here is a cool 3-dimensional effect that is quite simple to draw. It really will look like a cute square is rising off of the paper.

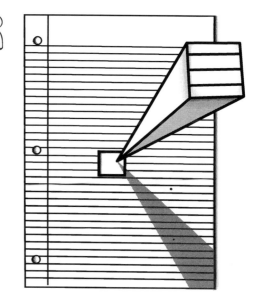

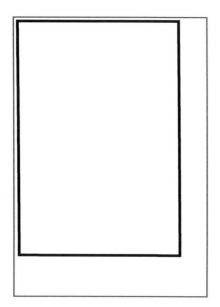

1. Draw a rectangle on the upper left side of a piece of paper.

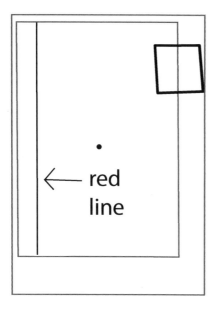

← red line

2. Draw a light red line along the left side of the rectangle. Draw slightly slanted rectangle on right side. Draw a dot on the page.

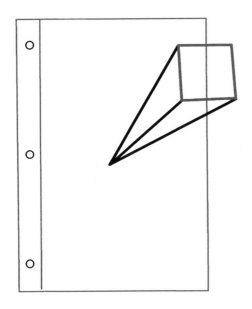

3. Draw lines from the rectangle down to the point you drew. Draw 3 circles on left side of page.

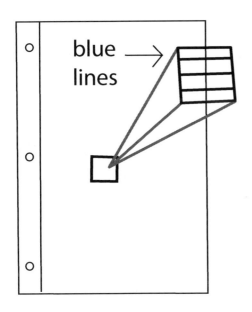

blue lines →

4. Draw a smaller rectangle around the point. Draw 3 blue lines on the bigger rectangle.

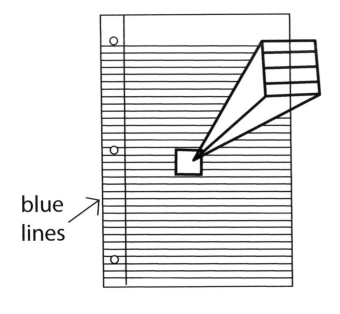

blue lines ↗

5. Draw blue lines around the shapes that you drew.

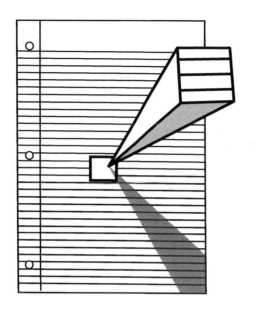

Draw a gray cast shadow by drawing 2 outward slanted lines that form a triangle. Fill it in gray. You should be able to see the lines thru the shadow. Use a lighter gray to shade the right side of the paper tower.

Shade the left side of the holes + rectangle

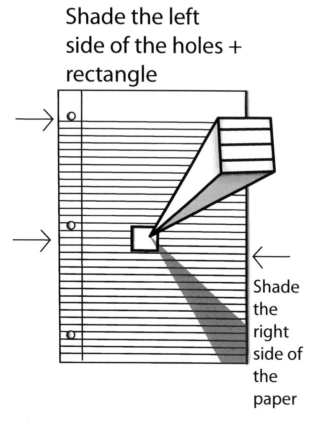

Shade the right side of the paper

Add some very light shading to the top of the paper tower. Add darker shading to the right side of the piece of paper, as well as the left side of the paper holes and the cut out rectangle.

GUY FALLING OFF YOUR PAPER

This is a cool drawing trick that will amaze your friends. It will actually look like a cartoon boy is hanging off of your paper. Find out how below.

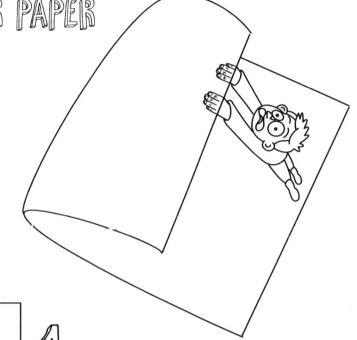

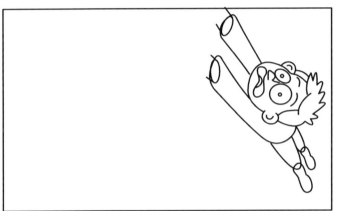

1. First of all, you need to draw a cartoon boy on the right side of a piece of paper turned on its side. We will show you how to draw him below.

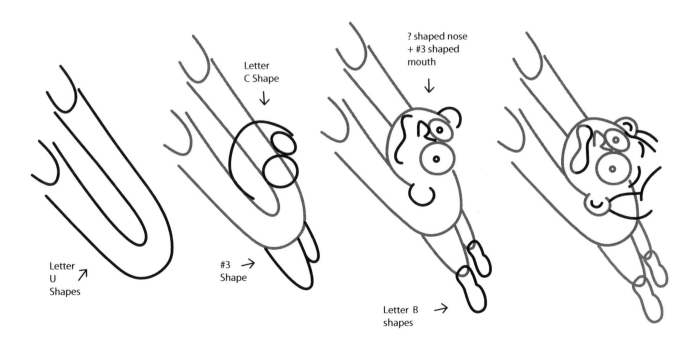

Letter U Shapes

#3 Shape

Letter C Shape

? shaped nose + #3 shaped mouth

Letter B shapes

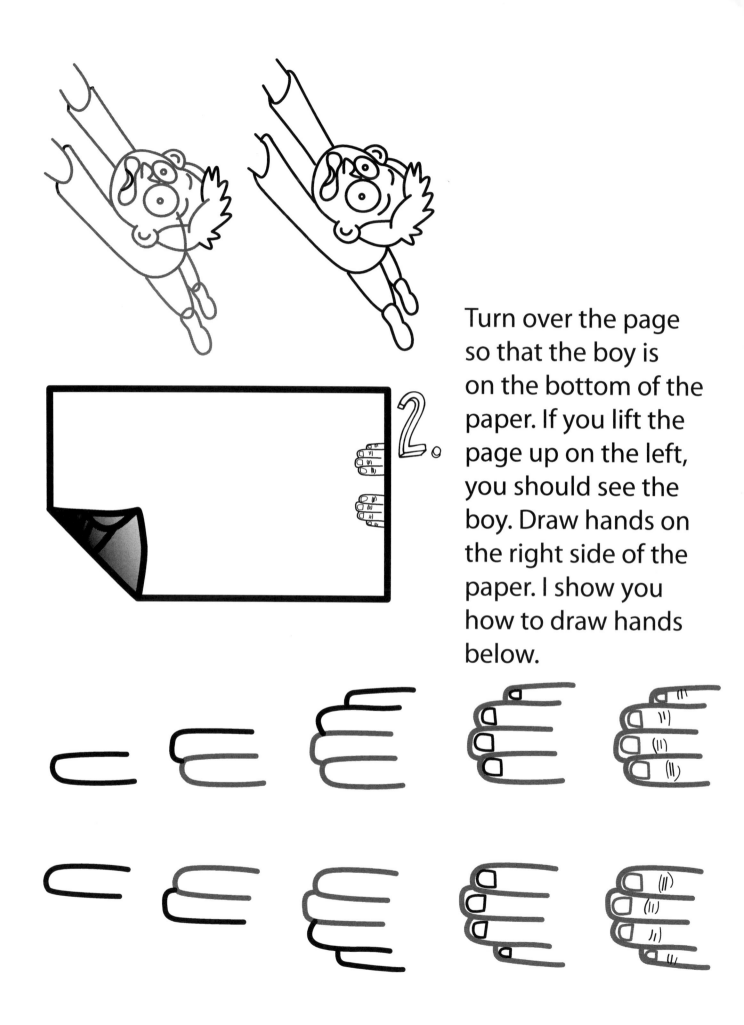

Turn over the page so that the boy is on the bottom of the paper. If you lift the page up on the left, you should see the boy. Draw hands on the right side of the paper. I show you how to draw hands below.

3. Now roll / curve the paper over and match up the hands with the arms. It will look like a 3d person is hanging off of your paper! Cool... isn't it?!!!

OUR OTHER BOOKS

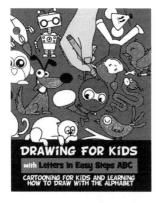

Please Give Us Good Reviews on Amazon! This book is self-published so we need to get the word out! **If You Give us a 5 Star Review**, and Email us About it, We Will Do a Tutorial Per Your Child's Request and Post it On DrawingHowToDraw.com

Made in the USA
Middletown, DE
24 October 2021